Common Core Lessons

Reading
Literary Text

Grade 1

Editorial Development: Barbara Allman
Lisa Vitarisi Mathews
Copy Editing: Laurie Westrich
Art Direction: Cheryl Puckett
Art Manager: Kathy Kopp
Cover Design: Yuki Meyer
Illustration: Ann Iosa
Cheryl Nobens
Design/Production: Carolina Caird
Jessica Onken
Marcia Smith

EMC 3211

Evan-Moor®
Helping Children Learn

Visit
teaching-standards.com
to view a correlation
of this book.
This is a free service.

Correlated to State and
Common Core State Standards

For information about other Evan-Moor products, call 1-800-777-4362,
fax 1-800-777-4332, or visit our Web site, www.evan-moor.com.
Entire contents © 2015 EVAN-MOOR CORP.
18 Lower Ragsdale Drive, Monterey, CA 93940-5746. Printed in USA.

CPSIA: Printed by McNaughton & Gunn, Saline, MI USA. [1/2015

Contents

What's in Every Unit?

Teacher Resource Pages provide lesson preparation and instructional guidance.

The unit overview includes:
- The guided reading level
- Lesson objectives
- A suggested learning path
- Common Core State Standards citations

The teaching path includes:
- A walk-through of each literary text selection and activity pages that support the unit

The close reading activity includes:
- Scripted questions and sample responses to inform and direct

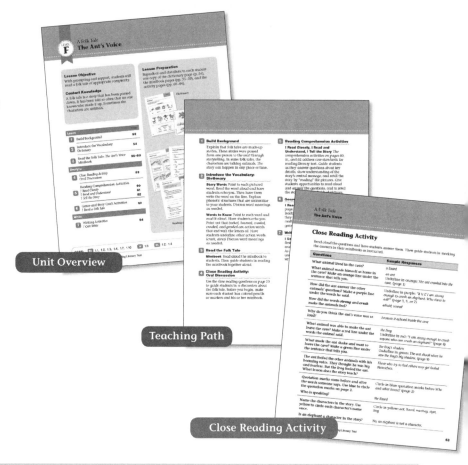

Unit Overview

Teaching Path

Close Reading Activity

Minibooks provide meaningful illustrations and accessible text.

Minibook

The stories and poems include a variety of fiction genres and provide a range of reading experiences.

Fiction genres include:
- Realistic Fiction
- Poetry
- Folk Tale
- Aesop's Fable
- Nursery Rhyme
- Historical Fiction

Student Pages help students understand vocabulary and focus on genre characteristics and literary elements.

Dictionary

A picture dictionary provides visual information for story vocabulary, helping students understand word meaning. The Words to Know lists additional vocabulary to introduce prior to reading the story or poem.

I Read Closely

A close reading activity presents students with pictures and sentences that ask students to connect text meaning and picture meaning.

I Read and Understand

A reading comprehension activity asks students to answer questions about the story, prompting them to examine it closely, and provides an informal assessment of students' understanding.

I Tell the Story

A retelling activity asks students to finish drawing the pictures and then use them to tell the story to someone.

I Read. . .

A genre study activity asks students text-based questions that focus on key ideas and details, craft and structure, and other literary elements.

I Can Write

A scaffolded writing activity asks students to complete sentences from the text and a text-based writing prompt.

Correlations:
Common Core State Standards

	Units							
RL **Reading Standards for Literature, Grade 1**	**Caleb's Year**	**Color**	**Bed in Summer**	**The Ant's Voice**	**The Bear and the Bees**	**Three Little Kittens**	**Mary's Fourth of July**	**Spider Woman**
Key Ideas and Details								
1.1 Ask and answer questions about key details in a text.	•	•	•	•	•	•	•	•
1.2 Retell stories, including key details, and demonstrate understanding of their central message or lesson.	•	•	•	•	•	•	•	•
1.3 Describe characters, settings, and major events in a story, using key details.	•	•	•	•	•	•	•	•
Craft and Structure								
1.4 Identify words and phrases in stories or poems that suggest feelings or appeal to the senses.		•	•	•	•	•		•
Integration of Knowledge and Ideas								
1.7 Use illustrations and details in a story to describe its characters, setting, or events.	•	•	•	•	•	•	•	•
Range of Reading and Level of Text Complexity								
1.10 With prompting and support, read prose and poetry of appropriate complexity for grade 1.	•	•	•	•	•	•	•	•

W **Writing Standards, Grade 1**								
Text Types and Purposes								
1.3 Write narratives in which they recount two or more appropriately sequenced events, include some details regarding what happened, use temporal words to signal event order, and provide some sense of closure.	•	•	•	•	•	•	•	•

SL **Speaking and Listening Standards, Grade 1**								
Comprehension and Collaboration								
1.2 Ask and answer questions about key details in a text read aloud or information presented orally or through other media.	•	•	•	•	•	•	•	•
Presentation of Knowledge and Ideas								
1.4 Describe people, places, things, and events with relevant details, expressing ideas and feelings clearly.	•	•	•	•	•	•	•	•

Correlations:
Texas Essential Knowledge and Skills

	Units							
110.12. English Language Arts and Reading, Grade 1	**Caleb's Year**	**Color**	**Bed in Summer**	**The Ant's Voice**	**The Bear and the Bees**	**Three Little Kittens**	**Mary's Fourth of July**	**Spider Woman**
110.12(b)(4) Reading/Beginning Reading/Strategies. Students comprehend a variety of texts drawing on useful strategies as needed. Students are expected to:								
(B) ask relevant questions, seek clarification, and locate facts and details about stories and other texts.	●	●	●	●	●	●	●	●
110.12(b)(6) Reading/Vocabulary Development. Students understand new vocabulary and use it when reading and writing. Students are expected to:								
(C) determine what words mean from how they are used in a sentence, either heard or read.	●	●	●	●	●	●	●	●
110.12(b)(7) Reading/Comprehension of Literary Text/Theme and Genre. Students analyze, make inferences and draw conclusions about theme and genre in different cultural, historical, and contemporary contexts and provide evidence from the text to support their understanding.	●	●	●	●	●	●	●	●
110.12 (b)(8) Reading/Comprehension of Literary Text/Poetry. Students understand, make inferences and draw conclusions about the structure and elements of poetry and provide evidence from text to support their understanding. Students are expected to respond to and use rhythm, rhyme, and alliteration in poetry.		●	●			●		
110.12 (b)(9) Reading/Comprehension of Literary Text/Fiction. Students understand, make inferences and draw conclusions about the structure and elements of fiction and provide evidence from text to support their understanding. Students are expected to:								
(A) describe the plot (problem and solution) and retell a story's beginning, middle, and end with attention to the sequence of events; and	●	●	●	●	●	●	●	●
(B) describe characters in a story and the reasons for their actions and feelings.				●	●	●	●	●

Overview of Texts

Title	Level	Genre	Literary Elements and Story Structure
Caleb's Year	D	Realistic Fiction	Time Order, Beginning, Middle, and End
Color, by Christina Rossetti	D	Poetry	Theme, Rhyme
Bed in Summer, by Robert Louis Stevenson	E	Poetry	Theme, Rhyme
The Ant's Voice	F	Folk Tale	Character, Plot
The Bear and the Bees	G	Aesop's Fable	Character, Plot
Three Little Kittens	H	Nursery Rhyme	Rhyme, Onomatopoeia
Mary's Fourth of July	H	Historical Fiction	Setting, Plot
Spider Woman	I	Navajo Folk Tale	Setting, Plot

Realistic Fiction
Caleb's Year

Lesson Objective

With prompting and support, students will read a realistic fiction story of appropriate complexity.

Content Knowledge

Realistic fiction is a made-up story that is written to represent real life. These stories help us to understand the world around us.

Lesson Preparation

Reproduce and distribute to each student one copy of the dictionary page (p. 12), the minibook pages (pp. 13–17), and the activity pages (pp. 18–22).

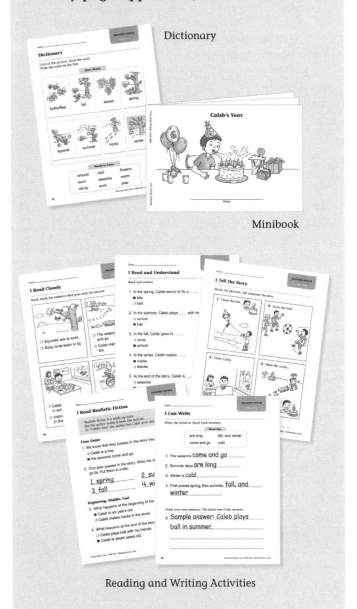

Dictionary

Minibook

Reading and Writing Activities

CCSS: **RL** 1.1, 1.2, 1.3, 1.7, 1.10   **W** 1.3   **SL** 1.2, 1.4

1 Build Background

Explain that realistic fiction is a made-up story, but it shows real life as it could be lived today. It is not based on history. The people in the story have normal human powers. Some events, people, and places in the story may even be real.

2 Introduce the Vocabulary: Dictionary

Story Words Point to each pictured word. Read the word aloud and have students echo you. Then have them write the word on the line. Explain phonetic structures that are unfamiliar to your students. Ask them to identify four words that name seasons of the year. (*fall, spring, summer, winter*) Have them circle those words. Discuss word meanings as needed.

Words to Know Point to each word and read it aloud. Have students echo you. Discuss word meanings as needed.

3 Read the Story

Minibook Read aloud the minibook to students. Then guide students in reading the minibook together aloud.

4 Close Reading Activity: Oral Discussion

Use the close reading questions on page 11 to guide students in a discussion about the story. Before you begin, make sure each student has colored pencils or markers and his or her minibook.

5 Reading Comprehension Activities

I Read Closely, I Read and Understand, I Tell the Story The comprehension activities on pages 18, 19, and 20 address core standards for reading literary text. Guide students as they answer questions about key details, show understanding of the story's central message, and retell the story by "reading" the pictures. Give students opportunities to read aloud and answer the questions, and to retell the story from their finished pictures.

6 Genre and Story Craft Activities

I Read Realistic Fiction The activities on page 21 address core standards for reading literary text. Guide students as they respond to questions about story craft and characteristics of the realistic fiction genre.

7 Writing Activities

I Can Write Guide students through the first writing activity on page 22. Then read aloud each completed sentence. As an informal assessment of students' understanding of the story, have them write a sentence describing one of the four seasons.

LEVEL D

Poetry
Color

© Evan-Moor Corp. • EMC 3211 • Reading Literary Text

Lesson Objective

With prompting and support, students will read a poem of appropriate complexity.

Content Knowledge

A poem is a collection of words that tell about an idea, a feeling, or an experience. Poems may have rhythm, rhyme, and repetition.

Lesson Preparation

Reproduce and distribute to each student one copy of the dictionary page (p. 26), the minibook pages (pp. 27–31), and the activity pages (pp. 32–36).

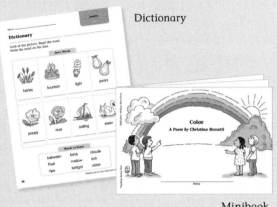

Dictionary

Minibook

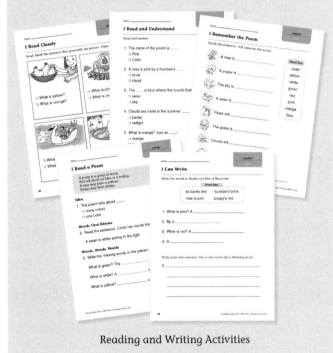

Reading and Writing Activities

CCSS: [RL] 1.1, 1.2, 1.3, 1.4, 1.7, 1.10 [W] 1.3 [SL] 1.2, 1.4

1 Build Background

Explain that the poem "Color" was written more than 100 years ago by a famous poet, Christina Rossetti. Tell students that poems may tell about ideas, feelings, or things that happen. This poem uses words that rhyme. It also has repetition, or words that are repeated over and over. Good poems make you see something you didn't see before, or see something in a new way. Sometimes people recite poems aloud.

2 Introduce the Vocabulary: Dictionary

Story Words Point to each pictured word. Read the word aloud and have students echo you. Then have them write the word on the line. Explain phonetic structures that are unfamiliar to your students. Ask them to listen for the sound at the end of *barley* and *poppy*. The letters *ey* and *y* stand for long *e*, /ē/. Have them circle the silent letters in *light: gh*. Discuss word meanings as needed. Ask them which word tells how something moves on water. (*sailing*)

Words to Know Point to each word and read it aloud. Have students echo you. Point out that *mellow, rich, ripe,* and *violet* are adjectives, or describing words. Discuss word meanings as needed.

3 Read the Poem

Minibook Read aloud the minibook to students. Before you begin, make sure each student has colored pencils or markers. Have students color the object that is referred to on each page as you read. Then guide students in reading the minibook together aloud.

4 Close Reading Activity: Oral Discussion

Use the close reading questions on page 25 to guide students in a discussion about the poem. Before you begin, make sure each student has colored pencils or markers and his or her minibook.

5 Reading Comprehension Activities

I Read Closely, I Read and Understand, I Remember the Poem The comprehension activities on pages 32, 33, and 34 address core standards for reading literary text. Guide students as they answer questions about key details, show understanding of the poem's central message, and remember parts of the poem by "reading" the pictures and words. Give students opportunities to read aloud and answer the questions, and to say the poem or the parts of the poem that they can remember.

6 Genre and Poetry Craft Activities

I Read a Poem The activities on page 35 address core standards for reading literary text. Guide students as they respond to questions about poetry craft and characteristics of the poetry genre.

7 Writing Activities

I Can Write Guide students through the first writing activity on page 36. Read aloud each completed line. Then reread aloud the completed verse. As an informal assessment of students' understanding of the poem, have them write a sentence that uses a color word and a word that rhymes with it.

Close Reading Activity

Read aloud the questions and have students answer them. Then guide students in marking the answers in their minibooks as instructed.

Questions	Sample Responses
What does the poet try to tell us in this poem? Make a line under the title of the poem using your favorite color.	*Colors are all around us.* Underline in favorite color: *Color* (front cover)
The word **rose** is another word for the color pink. The poet was having fun with this idea when she chose to write about a **pink** rose. Make a red line under the lines of the poem that tell about a rose.	Underline in red: *What is pink? A rose is pink / By a fountain's brink.* (page 1)
What does the poet want us to notice about the sky? Make a blue line under the words that tell you.	*She wants us to notice that the sky is blue and that there are clouds.* Underline in blue: *The sky is blue / Where the clouds float through.* (page 3)
What is special about the clouds in the sky?	Answers will vary.
Some pears change from green to yellow. According to the poem, when are they yellow? Make a yellow line under the words that tell you.	*When they are rich and ripe and mellow.* Underline in yellow: *Rich and ripe and mellow.* (page 5)
Which words tell us what else is in the grass? Make a green line under the words that tell you.	*small flowers* Underline in green: *With small flowers between.* (page 6)
How does the poet help us to see clouds of a different color than white? Make a purple line under the sentences.	Underline in purple: *What is violet? Clouds are violet / In the summer twilight.* (page 7)
Which thing in the poem has the same name as its color? Make an orange line under the sentences about it.	*an orange* Underline in orange: *What is orange? Why, an orange, / Just an orange!* (page 8)
What question is asked again and again in the poem?	*What is ____ (a color word)?*

Name: _____

Dictionary

Look at the picture. Read the word.
Write the word on the line.

Story Words

barley

_____

fountain

_____

light

_____

pears

_____

poppy

_____

rose

_____

sailing

_____

swan

_____

Words to Know

between	brink	clouds
float	mellow	rich
ripe	twilight	violet

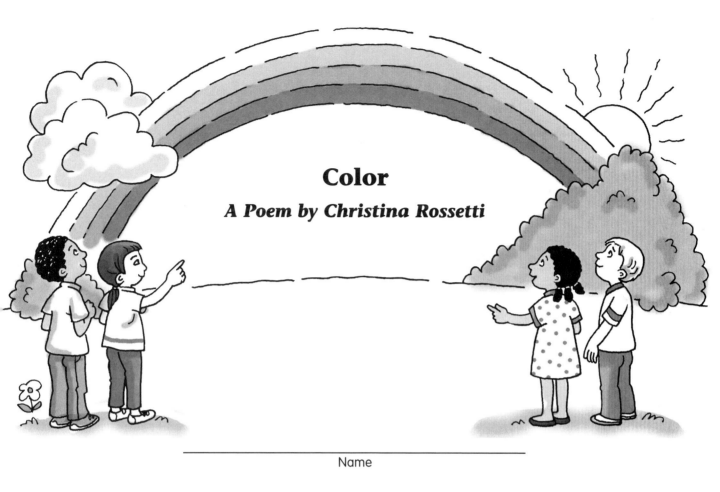

Color

A Poem by Christina Rossetti

Name

What is pink? A rose is pink
By a fountain's brink.

1

What is red? A poppy's red
In its barley bed.

What is blue? The sky is blue
Where the clouds float through.

What is white? A swan is white
Sailing in the light.

What is yellow? Pears are yellow,
Rich and ripe and mellow.

What is green? The grass is green,
With small flowers between.

What is violet? Clouds are violet
In the summer twilight.

What is orange? Why, an orange,
Just an orange!

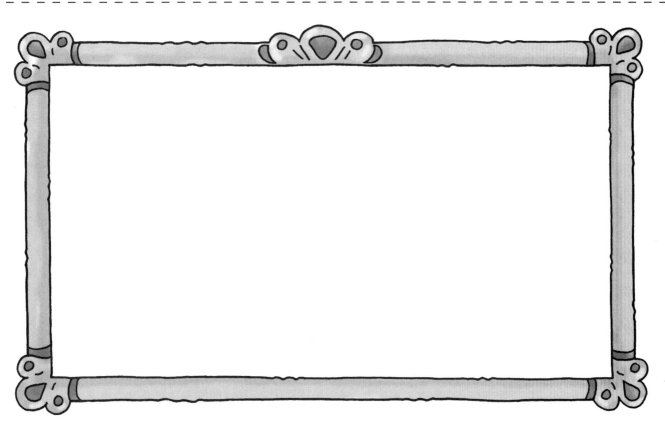

Draw a garden full of color.

Name: _____

I Read Closely

Read. Mark the sentence that goes with the picture. Then color.

○ What is yellow?

○ What is orange?

○ What is pink?

○ What is red?

○ What is violet?

○ What is white?

○ What is blue?

○ What is orange?

I Read and Understand

....

Read and answer.

1. The name of the poem is ____.
   - ○ Pink
   - ○ Color

2. A rose is pink by a fountain's ____.
   - ○ brink
   - ○ cloud

3. The ____ is blue where the clouds float through.
   - ○ swan
   - ○ sky

4. Clouds are violet in the summer ____.
   - ○ barley
   - ○ twilight

5. What is orange? Just an ____!
   - ○ orange
   - ○ pears

I Remember the Poem

Finish the sentences. Tell someone the poem.

 A rose is _____.

 A poppy is _____.

 The sky is _____.

 A swan is _____.

 Pears are _____.

 The grass is _____.

 Clouds are _____.

 An orange is _____.

Word Box

violet

yellow

white

green

red

pink

orange

blue

I told the poem to _____.

I Read a Poem

A poem is a group of words
that tell about an idea or a feeling.
Poems may have a pattern.
Poems may have rhyme.

Idea

1. The poem tells about ____.

   ○ many colors

   ○ one color

Words That Rhyme

2. Read the sentence. Circle two words that rhyme.

   A swan is white sailing in the light.

Words, Words, Words

3. Write the missing words in the pattern.

   What is green? The _____ is green.

   What is white? A _____ is white.

   What is yellow? _____ are yellow.

I Can Write

Write the words to finish each line of the poem.

Word Box

its barley bed	fountain's brink
rose is pink	poppy's red

1. What is pink? A _____

2. By a _____ .

3. What is red? A _____

4. In _____ .

Write your own sentence. Use a color word and a rhyming word.

5. _____

_____

_____

Poetry
Bed in Summer

Lesson Objective

With prompting and support, students will read a classic poem of appropriate complexity.

Content Knowledge

A poem is a collection of words that tell about an idea, a feeling, or an experience. Poems often have rhythm and sometimes use rhyme.

Lesson Preparation

Reproduce and distribute to each student one copy of the dictionary page (p. 40), the minibook pages (pp. 41–45), and the activity pages (pp. 46–50).

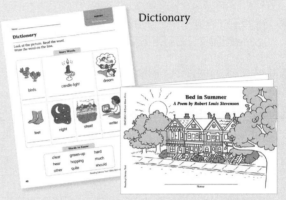

Dictionary

Minibook

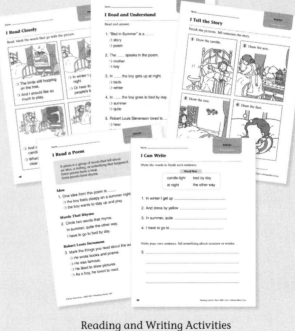

Reading and Writing Activities

CCSS: **RL** 1.1, 1.2, 1.3, 1.4, 1.7, 1.10 **W** 1.3 **SL** 1.2, 1.4

1 Build Background

Explain that the poem "Bed in Summer" was written more than 100 years ago by a famous author, Robert Louis Stevenson. Tell students that poems tell about ideas, feelings, or things that happen. Some poems have a beat. Some poems have rhyme. Poems may make you see something you didn't see before, or see something in a new way. Sometimes people recite poems aloud.

2 Introduce the Vocabulary: Dictionary

Story Words Point to each pictured word. Read the word aloud and have students echo you. Then have them write the word on the line. Explain phonetic structures that are unfamiliar to your students. Point out that the word *candle-light* has a hyphen that connects the two words *candle* and *light*. Ask them to listen for the long *i* sound of *igh* in *light* and *night*. Have them identify the letters *ea* and *ee* that stand for the long *e* sound in *dream, feet,* and *street*. Discuss word meanings as needed.

Words to Know Point to each word and read it aloud. Have students echo you. Point out that the word *grown-up* has a hyphen that connects the two words *grown* and *up*. Have students name the vowels they see in the word *quite*. (*u, i, e*) Then ask them to circle the one letter that stands for long *i*, /ī/. (the letter *i*) Discuss word meanings as needed.

3 Read the Poem

Minibook Read aloud the minibook to students. Then guide students in reading the minibook together aloud. Help students read the title, the genre, and the author's name on the cover and information about the author on the last page.

4 Close Reading Activity: Oral Discussion

Use the close reading questions on page 39 to guide students in a discussion about the poem. Before you begin, make sure each student has colored pencils or markers and his or her minibook.

5 Reading Comprehension Activities

I Read Closely, I Read and Understand, I Tell the Story The comprehension activities on pages 46, 47, and 48 address core standards for reading literary text. Guide students as they answer questions about key details, show understanding of the poem's central message, and retell the poem by "reading" the pictures. Give students opportunities to read aloud and answer the questions, and to tell about the poem from memory using their finished pictures.

6 Genre and Poetry Craft Activities

I Read a Poem The activities on page 49 address core standards for reading literary text. Guide students as they respond to questions about poetry craft and characteristics of the poetry genre.

7 Writing Activities

I Can Write Guide students through the first writing activity on page 50. Read aloud each completed line. Then reread aloud the completed verse. Give students an opportunity to clap the rhythm as they read. As an informal assessment of students' understanding of the poem, have them write a sentence to describe the season of their choosing.

Close Reading Activity

Read aloud the questions and have students answer them. Then guide students in marking the answers in their minibooks as instructed.

Questions	Sample Responses
What are winter mornings like for the boy in the poem? Make a brown line under the two lines of the poem that tell you.	*dark* Underline in brown: *In winter I get up at night / And dress by yellow candle-light.* (page 1)
How is summer different from winter?	*In summer, the boy goes to bed when it's light outside. In winter, the boy wakes up when it's dark outside.*
In summer, the sun sets later than in winter. Why does the boy say he has to "go to bed by day"?	*because he must go to bed before dark*
What does the boy see in the tree by his window? Make a red line under the line of the poem that tells you.	*He sees birds.* Underline in red: *The birds still hopping on the tree,* (page 3)
What does the boy hear outside his window when he goes to bed? Make a purple line under the two lines of the poem that tell you.	*He hears grown-ups walking around outside.* Underline in purple: *Or hear the grown-up people's feet / Still going past me in the street.* (page 4)
What is there about the sky that makes it hard to go to bed in summer? Make a green line under the line of the poem that tells you.	*The sky is blue and it's light outside.* Underline in green: *When all the sky is clear and blue,* (page 5)
What does the boy wish?	*He wishes he could play instead of going to bed.*
Robert Louis Stevenson could be the boy in the poem. Give a reason why this might be so. Highlight the sentences with yellow.	*When he was a boy he was sick and had to stay in bed.* Highlight in yellow: *He was often sick when he was a boy. Little Robert had to stay in bed.* (page 9)
Have you ever felt the way the boy in the poem does? If so, when?	Answers will vary.

Name: _____

Dictionary

Look at the picture. Read the word.
Write the word on the line.

Story Words

birds

_____

candle-light

_____

dream

_____

feet

_____

night

_____

street

_____

writer

_____

Words to Know

clear	grown-up	hard
hear	hopping	much
other	quite	should

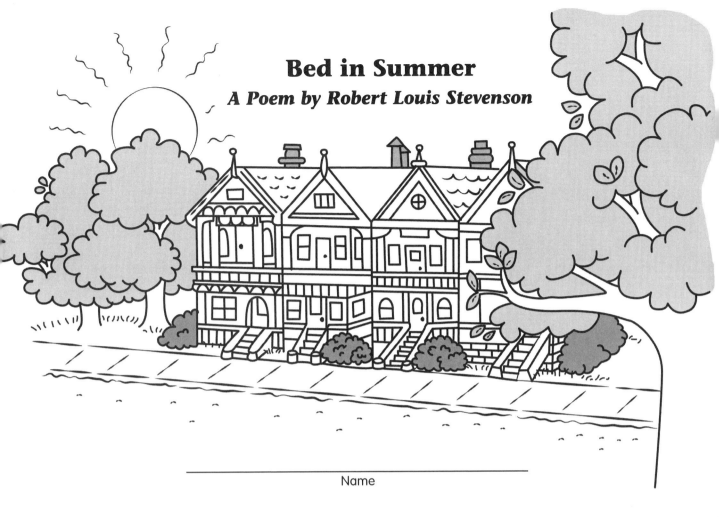

Bed in Summer
A Poem by Robert Louis Stevenson

Name _____

In winter I get up at night
And dress by yellow candle-light.

Reading Literary Text

1

In summer, quite the other way,
I have to go to bed by day.

I have to go to bed and see
The birds still hopping on the tree,

Or hear the grown-up people's feet
Still going past me in the street.

And does it not seem hard to you,
When all the sky is clear and blue,

And I should like so much to play,
To have to go to bed by day?

Draw your own dream.

Robert Louis Stevenson
was a famous writer.
He wrote books and poems.
He was often sick when
he was a boy.
Little Robert had to stay in bed.
But he loved to read stories.

Name: _____

I Read Closely

Read. Mark the words that go with the picture.

○ The birds still hopping on the tree,

○ And I should like so much to play,

○ In winter I get up at night

○ Or hear the grown-up people's feet

○ And dress by yellow candle-light.

○ When all the sky is clear and blue,

○ I have to go to bed by day.

○ And I should like so much to play,

Name: _____

I Read and Understand

Read and answer.

1. "Bed in Summer" is a ____.

   ○ story

   ○ poem

2. The ____ speaks in the poem.

   ○ mother

   ○ boy

3. In ____ the boy gets up at night.

   ○ birds

   ○ winter

4. In ____ the boy goes to bed by day.

   ○ summer

   ○ quite

5. Robert Louis Stevenson loved to ____.

   ○ hear

   ○ read

Name: _____

I Tell the Story

Finish the pictures. Tell someone the story.

1 Draw the candle.

2 Draw the sun.

3 Draw the tree.

4 Draw the face.

I told the story to _____.

Name: _____

I Read a Poem

A poem is a group of words that tell about
an idea, a feeling, or something that happened.
Some poems have a beat.
Some poems have rhyme.

Idea

1. One idea from this poem is ____.

   ○ the boy feels sleepy on a summer night

   ○ the boy wants to stay up and play

Words That Rhyme

2. Circle two words that rhyme.

   In summer, quite the other way,

   I have to go to bed by day.

Robert Louis Stevenson

3. Mark the things you read about the author of the poem.

   ○ He wrote books and poems.

   ○ He was famous.

   ○ He liked to draw pictures.

   ○ As a boy, he loved to read.

Name: _____

I Can Write

Write the words to finish each sentence.

Word Box

candle-light   bed by day

at night   the other way

1. In winter I get up _____

2. And dress by yellow _____.

3. In summer, quite _____,

4. I have to go to _____.

Write your own sentence. Tell something about summer or winter.

5. _____

_____

_____

_____

A Folk Tale
The Ant's Voice

Lesson Objective

With prompting and support, students will read a folk tale of appropriate complexity.

Content Knowledge

A folk tale is a story that has been passed down. It has been told so often that no one knows who made it up. Sometimes the characters are animals.

Lesson Preparation

Reproduce and distribute to each student one copy of the dictionary page (p. 54), the minibook pages (pp. 55–59), and the activity pages (pp. 60–64).

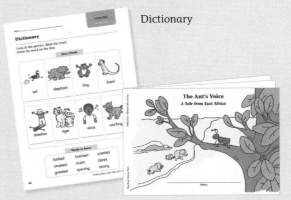

Dictionary

Minibook

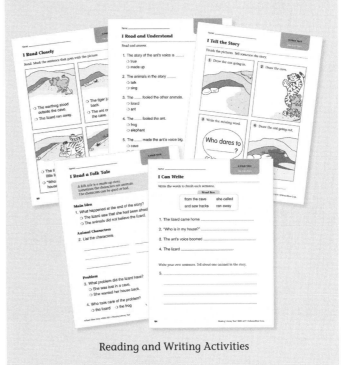

Reading and Writing Activities

CCSS: **RL** 1.1, 1.2, 1.3, 1.4, 1.7, 1.10   **W** 1.3   **SL** 1.2, 1.4

1 Build Background

Explain that folk tales are made-up stories. These stories were passed from one person to the next through storytelling. In some folk tales, the characters are talking animals. The story can happen in any place or time.

2 Introduce the Vocabulary: Dictionary

Story Words Point to each pictured word. Read the word aloud and have students echo you. Then have them write the word on the line. Explain phonetic structures that are unfamiliar to your students. Discuss word meanings as needed.

Words to Know Point to each word and read it aloud. Have students echo you. Point out that *barked, boomed, crawled, croaked,* and *growled* are action words that end with the letters *ed.* Have students underline other action words. (*crush, dares*) Discuss word meanings as needed.

3 Read the Folk Tale

Minibook Read aloud the minibook to students. Then guide students in reading the minibook together aloud.

4 Close Reading Activity: Oral Discussion

Use the close reading questions on page 53 to guide students in a discussion about the folk tale. Before you begin, make sure each student has colored pencils or markers and his or her minibook.

5 Reading Comprehension Activities

I Read Closely, I Read and Understand, I Tell the Story The comprehension activities on pages 60, 61, and 62 address core standards for reading literary text. Guide students as they answer questions about key details, show understanding of the story's central message, and retell the story by "reading" the pictures. Give students opportunities to read aloud and answer the questions, and to retell the story from their finished pictures.

6 Genre and Story Craft Activities

I Read a Folk Tale The activities on page 63 address core standards for reading literary text. Guide students as they respond to questions about story craft and characteristics of the folk tale genre.

7 Writing Activities

I Can Write Guide students through the first writing activity on page 64. Then read aloud each completed sentence. As an informal assessment of students' understanding of the story, have them write sentences about one character.

Close Reading Activity

Read aloud the questions and have students answer them. Then guide students in marking the answers in their minibooks as instructed.

Questions	Sample Responses
What animal lived in the cave?	*a lizard*
What animal made himself at home in the cave? Make an orange line under the sentence that tells you.	*an ant* Underline in orange: *The ant crawled into the cave.* (page 1)
How did the ant answer the other animals' questions? Make a purple line under the words he said.	Underline in purple: *"It is I! I am strong enough to crush an elephant. Who dares to ask?"* (page 3, 5, or 7)
How did the words **strong** and **crush** make the animals feel?	*afraid; scared*
Why do you think the ant's voice was so loud?	*because it echoed inside the cave*
What animal was able to make the ant leave the cave? Make a red line under the words the animal said.	*the frog* Underline in red: *"I am strong enough to crush anyone who can crush an elephant!"* (page 8)
What made the ant shake and want to leave the cave? Make a green line under the sentence that tells you.	*the frog's shadow* Underline in green: *The ant shook when he saw the frog's big shadow.* (page 9)
The ant fooled the other animals with his booming voice. They thought he was big and fearless. But the frog fooled the ant. What lesson does the story teach?	*Those who try to fool others may get fooled themselves.*
Quotation marks come before and after the words someone says. Use blue to circle the quotation marks on page 2.	Circle in blue: quotation marks before *Who* and after *house?* (page 2)
Who is speaking?	*the lizard*
Name the characters in the story. Use yellow to circle each character's name once.	Circle in yellow: *ant, lizard, warthog, tiger, frog*
Is an elephant a character in the story?	*No, an elephant is not a character.*

Dictionary

Look at the picture. Read the word.
Write the word on the line.

Story Words

ant

elephant

frog

lizard

shadow

tiger

voice

warthog

Words to Know

barked   boomed   crawled

croaked   crush   dares

growled   opening   strong

The Ant's Voice
A Tale from East Africa

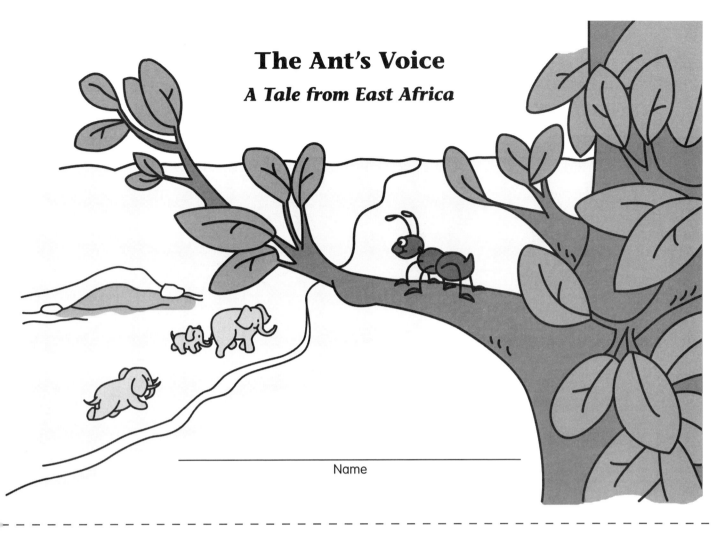

Name _____

Once upon a time an ant needed a new house.
The ant saw a cave. No one was home.
The ant crawled into the cave.

A lizard came home to the cave.
The lizard saw tracks.
"Who is in my house?" she called.

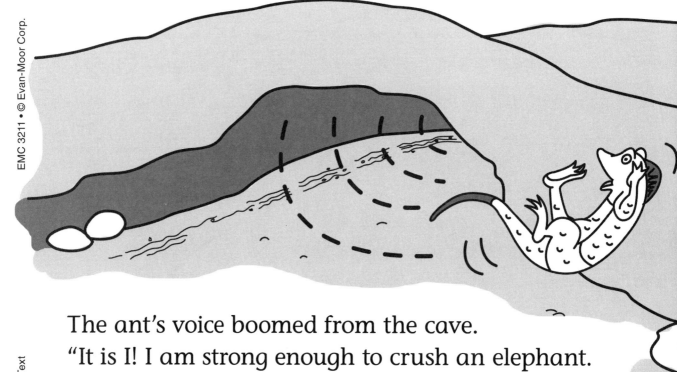

The ant's voice boomed from the cave.
"It is I! I am strong enough to crush an elephant.
Who dares to ask?"
The lizard ran away.

The lizard asked a warthog for help.
The warthog stood outside the cave.
"Who is in my friend's house?" he barked.

The ant's voice boomed from the cave.
"It is I! I am strong enough to crush an elephant.
Who dares to ask?"
The warthog ran away.

The lizard asked a tiger for help.
The tiger stood outside the cave.
"Who is in my friend's house?" she growled.

The ant's voice boomed from the cave.
"It is I! I am strong enough to crush an elephant.
Who dares to ask?"
The tiger jumped back.

The lizard asked a little frog for help.
The frog stood in the cave opening.
"I am strong enough to crush anyone who can crush
an elephant!" croaked the frog in a big voice.

The ant shook when he saw the frog's big shadow.
"I have had my fun," said the ant.
And the ant ran right out of the cave!

Name: _____

I Read Closely

Read. Mark the sentence that goes with the picture.

○ The warthog stood outside the cave.

○ The lizard ran away.

○ The tiger jumped back.

○ The ant crawled into the cave.

○ The lizard asked a little frog for help.

○ "Who is in my friend's house?" she growled.

○ "I have had my fun," said the ant.

○ The ant's voice boomed from the cave.

Name: _____

I Read and Understand

....

Read and answer.

1. The story of the ant's voice is ____.
   ○ true
   ○ made up

2. The animals in the story ____.
   ○ talk
   ○ sing

3. The ____ fooled the other animals.
   ○ lizard
   ○ ant

4. The ____ fooled the ant.
   ○ frog
   ○ elephant

5. The ____ made the ant's voice big.
   ○ cave
   ○ shadow

Name: _____

I Tell the Story

Finish the pictures. Tell someone the story.

1 Draw the ant going in.

2 Draw the cave.

3 Write the missing word.

Who dares to _____?

4 Draw the ant going out.

I told the story to _____.

Name: _____

I Read a Folk Tale

A folk tale is a made-up story.
Sometimes the characters are animals.
The characters can be good or bad.

Main Idea

1. What happened at the end of the story?

   ○ The lizard saw that she had been afraid of an ant.

   ○ The animals did not believe the lizard.

Animal Characters

2. List the characters.

   _____   _____

   _____   _____

   _____

Problem

3. What problem did the lizard have?

   ○ She was lost in a cave.

   ○ She wanted her house back.

4. Who took care of the problem?

   ○ the lizard   ○ the frog

© Evan-Moor Corp. • EMC 3211 • Reading Literary Text

63

Name: _____

I Can Write

Write the words to finish each sentence.

Word Box

| from the cave | she called |
| and saw tracks | ran away |

1. The lizard came home _____.

2. "Who is in my house?" _____.

3. The ant's voice boomed _____.

4. The lizard _____.

Write your own sentences. Tell about one animal in the story.

5. _____

_____

_____

_____

Aesop's Fable
The Bear and the Bees

Lesson Objective

With prompting and support, students will read a fable of appropriate complexity.

Content Knowledge

Some fables are stories that have been shared for thousands of years. Often, the characters are animals with human traits. Fables teach a lesson.

Lesson Preparation

Reproduce and distribute to each student one copy of the dictionary page (p. 68), the minibook pages (pp. 69–73), and the activity pages (pp. 74–78).

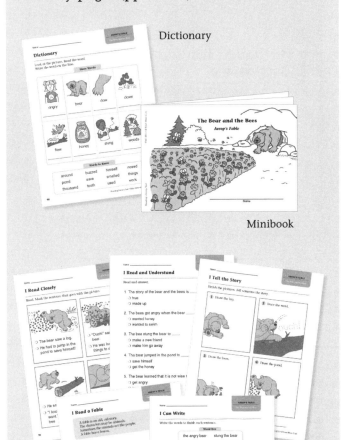

Dictionary

Minibook

Reading and Writing Activities

CCSS: **RL** 1.1, 1.2, 1.3, 1.4, 1.7, 1.10   **W** 1.3   **SL** 1.2, 1.4

1 Build Background

Explain that fables are made-up stories. Greek fables are thousands of years old. We do not know for certain if Aesop existed, but he is said to have been the author of *The Bear and the Bees*. In some fables, the characters are talking animals or objects. A fable teaches a lesson or moral.

2 Introduce the Vocabulary: Dictionary

Story Words Point to each pictured word. Read the word aloud and have students echo you. Then have them write the word on the line. Explain phonetic structures that are unfamiliar to your students. Ask them to listen for and name the blends at the beginning of *claw, clover, flew,* and *stung.* Discuss word meanings as needed.

Words to Know Point to each word and read it aloud. Have students echo you. Point out that *buzzed* ends with the letters *ed.* Have students underline three more vocabulary words with *ed.* (*nosed, smelled, used*) Have them find and circle the three words ending in *nd.* (*around, pond, thousand*) Discuss word meanings as needed.

3 Read the Fable

Minibook Read aloud the minibook to students. Then guide students in reading the minibook together aloud. Help them read and interpret the lesson on the last story page.

4 Close Reading Activity: Oral Discussion

Use the close reading questions on page 67 to guide students in a discussion about the fable. Before you begin, make sure each student has colored pencils or markers and his or her minibook.

5 Reading Comprehension Activities

I Read Closely, I Read and Understand, I Tell the Story The comprehension activities on pages 74, 75, and 76 address core standards for reading literary text. Guide students as they answer questions about key details, show understanding of the story's central message, and retell the story by "reading" the pictures. Give students opportunities to read aloud and answer the questions, and to retell the story from their finished pictures.

6 Genre and Story Craft Activities

I Read a Fable The activities on page 77 address core standards for reading literary text. Guide students as they respond to questions about story craft and characteristics of the fable genre.

7 Writing Activities

I Can Write Guide students through the first writing activity on page 78. Then read aloud each completed sentence. As an informal assessment of students' understanding of the story, have them write a sentence telling the lesson learned by the bear in the fable.

Close Reading Activity

Read aloud the questions and have students answer them. Then guide students in marking the answers in their minibooks as instructed.

Questions	Sample Responses
Where does the story take place? Make a brown line under the sentence that tells where.	*in the woods* Underline in brown: *A bear went into the woods one day.* (page 1)
Why did the bear nose around the log? Make a blue line under the sentence that tells why.	*The bear smelled honey.* Underline in blue: *He smelled honey!* (page 2)
What did the bee say when she saw the bear? Make a yellow circle around the bee's words.	Circle in yellow: *"I know what you want,"* (page 5)
How do you know they are the bee's words?	*Quotation marks come before and after the words.*
Did the bee want the bear to get the honey? How do you know? Make a red line under the sentence that tells what happened.	*No. The bee stung the bear to stop him from getting the honey.* Underline in red: *The bee flew at the bear and stung him.* (page 6)
What words tell you the bear was hurt and angry after he was stung?	*"Ouch!" said the angry bear.*
What did he do next? Make a green line under the sentence that tells you.	*He tore apart the log to get to the honey.* Underline in green: *He used tooth and claw to get the nest.* (page 7)
Was the bear wise to try to get the nest? What happened next? Make a purple line under the sentence that tells you.	*No, the bees flew out and got angry.* Underline in purple: *Then all of the bees flew out.* (page 7)
How did the bear save himself?	*He ran away and jumped into the pond.*
The bear caused himself even more trouble by getting angry. What lesson does this fable teach?	*Sometimes getting angry makes things worse. It is wiser to put up with one hurt than to get angry and cause a thousand.* (page 9)
Can you think of a time in your own life when this lesson could have helped you?	Answers will vary.

Dictionary

Look at the picture. Read the word.
Write the word on the line.

Story Words

angry

_____

bear

_____

claw

_____

clover

_____

flew

_____

honey

_____

stung

_____

woods

_____

Words to Know

around	buzzed	himself	nosed
pond	save	smelled	things
thousand	tooth	used	work

The Bear and the Bees

Aesop's Fable

Name _____

A bear went into the woods one day.
He was looking for things to eat.

The bear saw a log.
He smelled honey!

The bear nosed around the log.
"The bees are not home," he said to himself.

Just then a bee flew home from work.
She had been in the clover.

The bee saw the bear.
"I know what you want," buzzed the bee.

The bee flew at the bear and stung him.
Then the bee flew into the log.

"Ouch!" said the angry bear.
He used tooth and claw to get the nest.
Then all of the bees flew out.

The bear had to run to get away.
He had to jump in the pond to save himself!

Lesson: *It is wiser to put up with one hurt than to get angry and cause a thousand.*

I Read Closely

Read. Mark the sentence that goes with the picture.

○ The bear saw a log.

○ He had to jump in the pond to save himself!

○ "Ouch!" said the angry bear.

○ He was looking for things to eat.

○ He smelled honey!

○ "I know what you want," buzzed the bee.

○ She had been in the clover.

○ The bee flew at the bear and stung him.

Name: _____

I Read and Understand

Read and answer.

1. The story of the bear and the bees is _____.

   ○ true

   ○ made up

2. The bees got angry when the bear _____.

   ○ wanted honey

   ○ wanted to swim

3. The bee stung the bear to _____.

   ○ make a new friend

   ○ make him go away

4. The bear jumped in the pond to _____.

   ○ save himself

   ○ get the honey

5. The bear learned that it is not wise to _____.

   ○ get angry

   ○ jump in the water

Name: _____

I Tell the Story

Finish the pictures. Tell someone the story.

1 Draw the log.

2 Trace the word.

3 Draw the bees.

4 Draw the pond.

I told the story to _____.

I Read a Fable

A fable is an old, old story.
The characters may be animals.
Sometimes the animals act like people.
A fable has a lesson.

Lesson

1. The bear learned that _____.

   ○ bears should not eat bees

   ○ getting angry makes things worse

Characters

2. Who are the story characters?

   _____   _____

3. Who got angry at the bees? _____

4. Who got angry at the bear? _____

Cause and Effect

5. Mark the things that happened because the bear got angry.

   ○ The bear had to jump in the pond to save himself.

   ○ The bear got the honey.

   ○ All the bees flew at the bear.

   ○ The bear went into the woods.

I Can Write

Write the words to finish each sentence.

Word Box

the angry bear	stung the bear
run away	to get the nest

1. The bee _____.

2. "Ouch!" said _____.

3. The angry bear wanted _____.

4. The bear had to _____.

Write your own sentence. Tell what the bear learned.

5. _____

_____

_____

_____

A Nursery Rhyme
Three Little Kittens

LEVEL H

Lesson Objective

With prompting and support, students will read a nursery rhyme of appropriate complexity.

Content Knowledge

Nursery rhymes are very old rhymes written for children. Many of them tell a story. Nursery rhymes have different authors, but people like to say that they were all written by a made-up person, Mother Goose.

Lesson Preparation

Reproduce and distribute to each student one copy of the dictionary page (p. 82), the minibook pages (pp. 83–87), and the activity pages (pp. 88–92).

Dictionary

Minibook

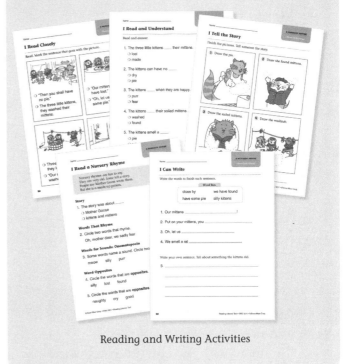

Reading and Writing Activities

CCSS: **RL** 1.1, 1.2, 1.3, 1.4, 1.7, 1.10   **W** 1.3   **SL** 1.2, 1.4

1 Build Background

Explain that nursery rhymes are very old rhymes that were written for children. They are fun to say. Many nursery rhymes tell a story. Nursery rhymes have many different authors, but people like to say that they were all written by a made-up person named Mother Goose.

2 Introduce the Vocabulary: Dictionary

Story Words Point to each pictured word. Read the word aloud and have students echo you. Then have them write the word on the line. Explain phonetic structures that are unfamiliar to your students. Point out that *kittens* and *mittens* rhyme. The two words have the same letters except for the first letter. Discuss word meanings as needed.

Words to Know Point to each word and read it aloud. Have students echo you. Point out that *meow* is a word made from the sound a kitten makes. That kind of word is called *onomatopoeia*. Have students give a sigh and listen to the sound. Do they think *sigh* is another example of onomatopoeia? Discuss word meanings as needed.

3 Read the Nursery Rhyme

Minibook Read aloud the minibook to students. Then guide students in reading the minibook together aloud.

4 Close Reading Activity: Oral Discussion

Use the close reading questions on page 81 to guide students in a discussion about the nursery rhyme. Before you begin, make sure each student has colored pencils or markers and his or her minibook.

5 Reading Comprehension Activities

I Read Closely, I Read and Understand, I Tell the Story The comprehension activities on pages 88, 89, and 90 address core standards for reading literary text. Guide students as they answer questions about key details, show understanding of the nursery rhyme's central message, and retell the story by "reading" the pictures. Give students opportunities to read aloud together, and to retell the story from their finished pictures using the original language of the rhyme where they are able.

6 Genre and Story Craft Activities

I Read a Nursery Rhyme The activities on page 91 address core standards for reading literary text. Guide students as they respond to questions about story craft and characteristics of the nursery rhyme genre.

7 Writing Activities

I Can Write Guide students through the first writing activity on page 92. Then read aloud each completed sentence. As an informal assessment of students' understanding of the nursery rhyme, have them write a sentence to describe something the main characters did.

Close Reading Activity

Read aloud the questions and have students answer them. Then guide students in marking the answers in their minibooks as instructed.

Questions	Sample Responses
What did the three little kittens tell their mother at the beginning of the story? Make a red line under the sentence that tells you.	*They lost their mittens.* Underline in red: *"Oh, mother dear, we sadly fear / Our mittens we have lost."* (page 1)
What words tell you how they feel?	*cry, sadly fear*
How did the kittens earn some pie after they lost their mittens? Make a purple line under the words that tell you.	*They found their mittens.* Underline in purple: *The three little kittens, they found their mittens,* (page 3)
What did the kittens wear while they ate? Make an orange line under the sentence that tells you.	*They wore their mittens.* Underline in orange: *The three little kittens put on their mittens, / And soon ate up the pie.* (page 5)
What did the kittens' mother call them after they soiled their mittens?	*She called them naughty.*
Look at the picture on page 6. What does it tell you about how the kittens feel?	Answers will vary.
What did the kittens' mother say after they washed their mittens? Make a green line under the words that tell you.	*She said they were good.* Underline in green: *"What! washed your mittens, then you're good kittens,"* (page 8)
At the end of the story, who do you think came looking for some leftover pie?	*The rat, because the picture shows it peeking around the door at what's left of the pie.*
The kittens' mother taught them how to smell a rat. Make a brown line under the words she used.	Underline in brown: *"But I smell a rat close by."* (page 8)
Who are the five animal characters?	*The five characters are the three kittens, the kittens' mother, and the rat.*
Which one does not speak? Draw a green circle around its picture.	*The rat does not speak.* Circle in green the rat on page 8 or 9.

Name: _____

Dictionary

Look at the picture. Read the word.
Write the word on the line.

Story Words

hear

kittens

mittens

naughty

_____

_____

_____

_____

pie

silly

soiled

washed

_____

_____

_____

_____

Words to Know

cry	dear	fear	found
greatly	hung	lost	meow
sadly	shall	sigh	

Three Little Kittens

by Mother Goose

_____
Name

Three little kittens, they lost their mittens,
And they began to cry,
"Oh, mother dear, we sadly fear
Our mittens we have lost."

1

"What! lost your mittens, you naughty kittens!
Then you shall have no pie."
"Meow, meow, meow."
"No, you shall have no pie."

The three little kittens, they found their mittens,
And they began to cry,
"Oh, mother dear, see here, see here,
Our mittens we have found!"

"Put on your mittens, you silly kittens,
And you shall have some pie."
"Purr, purr, purr,
Oh, let us have some pie."

4

The three little kittens put on their mittens,
And soon ate up the pie.
"Oh, mother dear, we greatly fear
Our mittens we have soiled."

5

"What! soiled your mittens, you naughty kittens!"
Then they began to sigh,
"Meow, meow, meow."
Then they began to sigh.

The three little kittens, they washed their mittens,
And hung them out to dry.
"Oh, mother dear, do you not hear,
Our mittens we have washed!"

"What! washed your mittens, then you're good kittens,
But I smell a rat close by."
"Meow, meow, meow.
We smell a rat close by."

8

THE END

9

Name: _____

I Read Closely

Read. Mark the sentence that goes with the picture.

○ "Then you shall have no pie."

○ The three little kittens, they washed their mittens.

○ "Our mittens we have lost."

○ "Oh, let us have some pie."

○ Three little kittens, they lost their mittens.

○ "Our mittens we have washed!"

○ "Purr, purr, purr."

○ "We smell a rat close by."

Reading Literary Text • EMC 3211 • © Evan-Moor Corp

Name: _____

I Read and Understand

Read and answer.

1. The three little kittens ____ their mittens.

   ○ lost

   ○ made

2. The kittens can have no ____.

   ○ dry

   ○ pie

3. The kittens ____ when they are happy.

   ○ purr

   ○ fear

4. The kittens ____ their soiled mittens.

   ○ washed

   ○ found

5. The kittens smell a ____.

   ○ pie

   ○ rat

Name: _____

I Tell the Story

Finish the pictures. Tell someone the story.

1 Draw the pie.

2 Draw the found mittens.

3 Draw the soiled mittens.

4 Draw the washtub.

I told the story to _____.

Name: _____

I Read a Nursery Rhyme

Nursery rhymes are fun to say.
They are very old. Some tell a story.
People say Mother Goose wrote them.
But she is a made-up person.

Story

1. The story was about _____.

   ○ Mother Goose

   ○ kittens and mittens

Words That Rhyme

2. Circle two words that rhyme.

   Oh, mother dear, we sadly fear

Words for Sounds: Onomatopoeia

3. Some words name a sound. Circle two kitten sounds.

   meow   silly   purr

Word Opposites

4. Circle the words that are **opposites**.

   silly   lost   found

5. Circle the words that are **opposites**.

   naughty   cry   good

I Can Write

Write the words to finish each sentence.

Word Box	
close by	we have found
have some pie	silly kittens

1. Our mittens _____!

2. Put on your mittens, you _____.

3. Oh, let us _____.

4. We smell a rat _____.

Write your own sentence. Tell about something the kittens did.

5. _____

_____

_____

_____

Historical Fiction
Mary's Fourth of July

Lesson Objective
With prompting and support, students will read a fiction story of appropriate complexity that is set in the past.

Content Knowledge
Fiction is a story that is make-believe. Historical fiction is a story that takes place in the past and includes some real people, places, or events.

Lesson Preparation
Reproduce and distribute to each student one copy of the dictionary page (p. 96), the minibook pages (pp. 97–101), and the activity pages (pp. 102–106).

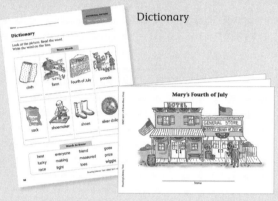

Dictionary

Minibook

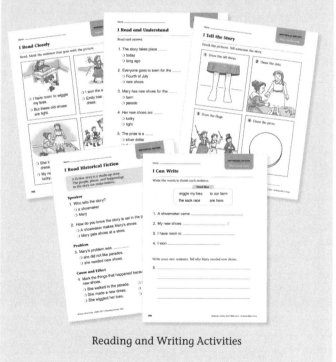

Reading and Writing Activities

CCSS: RL 1.1, 1.2, 1.3, 1.7, 1.10   W 1.3   SL 1.2, 1.4

1 Build Background

Explain that fiction stories are made up. These stories have make-believe characters. The things that happen are also made up. The place where the story happens might be made up or real. Historical fiction stories take place long ago.

2 Introduce the Vocabulary: Dictionary

Story Words Point to each pictured word. Read the word aloud and have students echo you. Then have them write the word on the line. Explain phonetic structures that are unfamiliar to your students. Draw their attention to the word *shoe* in *shoes* and *shoemaker*. Discuss word meanings as needed.

Words to Know Point to each word and read it aloud. Have students echo you. Point out that in the word *tight*, the letters *g* and *h* are silent. The letter *e* is silent at the end of *prize*. Have students underline three more vocabulary words with silent *e* at the end. (*everyone, race, wiggle*) Discuss word meanings as needed.

3 Read the Story

Minibook Read aloud the minibook to students. Then guide students in reading the minibook together aloud.

4 Close Reading Activity: Oral Discussion

Use the close reading questions on page 95 to guide students in a discussion about the story. Before you begin, make sure each student has colored pencils or markers and his or her minibook.

5 Reading Comprehension Activities

I Read Closely, I Read and Understand, I Tell the Story The comprehension activities on pages 102, 103, and 104 address core standards for reading literary text. Guide students as they answer questions about key details, show understanding of the story's central message, and retell the story by "reading" the pictures. Give students opportunities to read aloud and answer the questions, and to retell the story from their finished pictures.

6 Genre and Story Craft Activities

I Read Historical Fiction The activities on page 105 address core standards for reading literary text. Guide students as they respond to questions about story craft and characteristics of the historical fiction genre.

7 Writing Activities

I Can Write Guide students through the first writing activity on page 106. Then read aloud each completed sentence. As an informal assessment of students' understanding of the story, have them write a sentence to tell why Mary needed new shoes.

Close Reading Activity

Read aloud the questions and have students answer them. Then guide students in marking the answers in their minibooks as instructed.

Questions	Sample Responses
Who is telling the story? Make an orange circle around the person's picture.	*Mary is telling the story.* Circle in orange: Mary's picture (page 1)
How does Mary describe her shoes at the beginning of the story? Make a blue line under the sentence that tells you.	*She said they were old and tight.* Underline in blue: *But these old shoes are tight.* (page 1)
Why does Mary want new shoes? Make a red line under the sentence that tells you.	*She is going to walk in a parade.* Underline in red: *I am going to walk in the parade.* (page 1)
Why did Emily's mother measure and cut cloth? Make a purple line under the sentences that tell you.	*She needed to make Emily a new dress for the parade.* Underline in purple: *She is making a new dress. Emily will have it for the parade.* (page 4)
How do you know Mary's new shoes fit her better than the old ones? Make a blue line under the sentence that tells you.	*She had room to wiggle her toes.* Underline in blue: *I have room to wiggle my toes.* (page 5)
What things happened at a Fourth of July celebration long ago? Compare this with a Fourth of July celebration today.	*There was a parade. There were games. One game was the sack race. There were prizes, too.* Comparisons will vary.
Why does Mary say her new shoes are lucky? Make a green line under the sentences that tell you.	She won the sack race. Underline in green: *I won the sack race. The prize was one silver dollar!* (pages 8, 9)
This story takes place long ago in the past. It is a historical fiction story. Explain how Mary got her new shoes. Look at the pictures for clues.	*A shoemaker came to the farm where she lived. He measured her feet. Then he sent Mary the shoes in the mail.*
How do people today get new shoes?	*Today, people buy shoes in a store or order them online.*

Name: _____

Dictionary

Look at the picture. Read the word.
Write the word on the line.

Story Words

cloth

_____

farm

_____

Fourth of July

_____

parade

_____

sack

_____

shoemaker

_____

shoes

_____

silver dollar

_____

Words to Know

best	everyone	friend	goes
lucky	making	measured	prize
race	tight	toes	wiggle

Mary's Fourth of July

_____
Name

The Fourth of July is coming!
I am going to walk in the parade.
But these old shoes are tight.

A shoemaker came to our farm.
He measured my feet.
He will make my new shoes.

- -

The Fourth of July will be fun.
Everyone goes to town.
My best friend Emily will be there.

Emily's mother measured and cut some cloth.
She is making a new dress.
Emily will have it for the parade.

It is Thursday.
My new shoes are here!
I have room to wiggle my toes.

Emily has a new dress.
I have new shoes.
We are ready for the Fourth of July parade.

It is Friday, the Fourth of July!
Emily and I walk in the parade.
Later, there are games and prizes.

My new shoes are lucky.
I won the sack race.

The prize was one silver dollar!

I Read Closely

Read. Mark the sentence that goes with the picture.

- ○ I have room to wiggle my toes.
- ○ But these old shoes are tight.

- ○ I won the sack race.
- ○ Emily has a new dress.

- ○ She is making a new dress.
- ○ My new shoes are lucky.

- ○ Everyone goes to town.
- ○ Emily and I walk in the parade.

I Read and Understand

Read and answer.

1. The story takes place _____.
   - ○ today
   - ○ long ago

2. Everyone goes to town for the _____.
   - ○ Fourth of July
   - ○ new shoes

3. Mary has new shoes for the _____.
   - ○ farm
   - ○ parade

4. Her new shoes are _____.
   - ○ lucky
   - ○ tight

5. The prize is a _____.
   - ○ silver dollar
   - ○ dress

I Tell the Story

Finish the pictures. Tell someone the story.

1 Draw the old shoes.

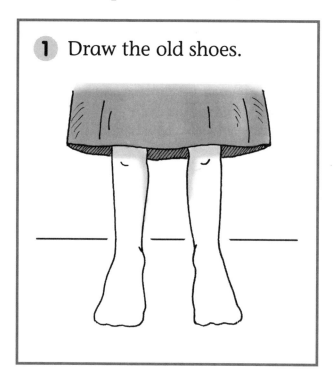

2 Draw the dots.

3 Draw the flags.

4 Draw the prize.

I told the story to _____.

I Read Historical Fiction

A fiction story is a made-up story.
The people, places, and happenings
in the story are make-believe.

Speaker

1. Who tells the story?
   - ○ a shoemaker
   - ○ Mary

2. How do you know the story is set in the past?
   - ○ A shoemaker makes Mary's shoes.
   - ○ Mary gets shoes at a store.

Problem

3. Mary's problem was _____.
   - ○ she did not like parades
   - ○ she needed new shoes

Cause and Effect

4. Mark the things that happened because Mary got new shoes.
   - ○ She walked in the parade.
   - ○ She made a new dress.
   - ○ She wiggled her toes.
   - ○ She was sad.
   - ○ She had fun.
   - ○ She won a prize.

I Can Write

Write the words to finish each sentence.

Word Box

wiggle my toes	to our farm
the sack race	are here

1. A shoemaker came _____.

2. My new shoes _____!

3. I have room to _____.

4. I won _____.

Write your own sentence. Tell why Mary needed new shoes.

5. _____

_____

_____

_____

A Navajo Folk Tale
Spider Woman

Lesson Objective
With prompting and support, students will read a folk tale of appropriate complexity.

Content Knowledge
A folk tale is a story that has been passed down. It may be about an actual place or thing. Some folk tales have an element of magic. Sometimes folk tale characters are animals.

Lesson Preparation
Reproduce and distribute to each student one copy of the dictionary page (p. 110), the minibook pages (pp. 111–115), and the activity pages (pp. 116–120).

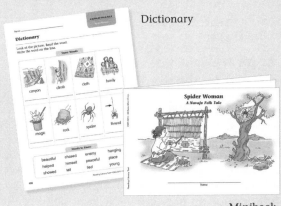

Dictionary

Minibook

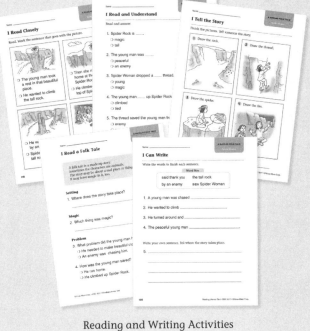

Reading and Writing Activities

CCSS: 1.1, 1.2, 1.3, 1.4, 1.7, 1.10   1.3   SL 1.2, 1.4

1 Build Background

Explain that folk tales are made-up stories. These stories were passed from person to person through storytelling. In some folk tales, the characters are animals. Some folk tales, like this Navajo legend, have something magical in the story.

2 Introduce the Vocabulary: Dictionary

Story Words Point to each pictured word. Read the word aloud and have students echo you. Then have them write the word on the line. Explain phonetic structures that are unfamiliar to your students. Ask them to listen for the sound of hard c /k/ in *canyon, climb, cloth, magic,* and *rock*. Discuss word meanings as needed.

Words to Know Point to each word and read it aloud. Have students echo you. Point out that *place* ends with the sound of soft c /s/. Have students listen for soft c and underline the letter c in the medial position in the word *peaceful*. Discuss word meanings as needed.

3 Read the Folk Tale

Minibook Read aloud the minibook to students. Then guide students in reading the minibook together aloud.

4 Close Reading Activity: Oral Discussion

Use the close reading questions on page 109 to guide students in a discussion about the folk tale. Before you begin, make sure each student has colored pencils or markers and his or her minibook.

5 Reading Comprehension Activities

I Read Closely, I Read and Understand, I Tell the Story The comprehension activities on pages 116, 117, and 118 address core standards for reading literary text. Guide students as they answer questions about key details, show understanding of the story's central message, and retell the story by "reading" the pictures. Give students opportunities to read aloud and answer the questions, and to retell the story from their finished pictures.

6 Genre and Story Craft Activities

I Read a Folk Tale The activities on page 119 address core standards for reading literary text. Guide students as they respond to questions about story craft and characteristics of the folk tale genre.

7 Writing Activities

I Can Write Guide students through the first writing activity on page 120. Then read aloud each completed sentence. As an informal assessment of students' understanding of the story, have them write a sentence to describe the setting of the story.

Close Reading Activity

Read aloud the questions and have students answer them. Then guide students in marking the answers in their minibooks as instructed.

Questions	Sample Responses
What words tell us about the setting of the story?	*tall rock, canyon*
Both a spider web and cloth are woven from threads. What did Spider Woman teach the people to do? Make an orange line under the sentence that tells you.	*She taught them how to make cloth.* Underline in orange: *She showed them how to make beautiful cloth.* (page 2)
The young man did not want to fight. Which word describes someone who tries not to fight? Make a green circle around the word.	*peaceful* Circle in green: *peaceful* (pages 3, 9)
At first, did the young man think he could climb up Spider Rock? Make a red line under the sentence that tells you.	*No, he thought the rock was too tall.* Underline in red: *"The rock is too tall," he said to himself.* (page 4)
What magically appeared to help the young man? Make a purple line under the sentence that tells you.	*a thread* Underline in purple: *Then he saw a thread.* (page 5)
How did the young man use the magic thread? Make a yellow line under the three sentences that tell you.	*He used it to climb to the top of Spider Rock.* Underline in yellow: *The young man took hold of the magic thread. He tied it around himself. He climbed up to the top of Spider Rock.* (page 6)
Who had put the magic thread there? Make a blue X on the page that tells how she did it.	*Spider Woman* Make a blue X beside: *The young man turned around and saw Spider Woman. Her thread had saved him. She had tied one end to a rock. Then she dropped the other end to the ground.* (page 8)
After he said thank you and ran home, what did the young man do? Make a green line under the sentence that tells you.	*He told his family about Spider Woman.* Underline in green: *He told his family how Spider Woman had saved him.* (page 9)

Name: _____

Dictionary

Look at the picture. Read the word.
Write the word on the line.

Story Words

canyon

_____

climb

_____

cloth

_____

family

_____

magic

_____

rock

_____

spider

_____

thread

_____

Words to Know

beautiful	chased	enemy	hanging
helped	himself	peaceful	place
showed	tell	tied	young

Spider Woman
A Navajo Folk Tale

_____
Name

Spider Rock is a tall, tall rock in a canyon.
The people who live by the rock tell this story.

1

Long ago, Spider Woman helped the people.
She showed them how to make beautiful cloth.
Then she made her home at the top of Spider Rock.

One day, there was a peaceful young man.
He was being chased by an enemy.
He ran into the canyon to get away.

The young man looked up and saw Spider Rock.
He wanted to climb the tall rock.
"The rock is too tall," he said to himself.

Then he saw a thread. It was like magic.
The thread was hanging down from the tall rock.

The young man took hold of the magic thread.
He tied it around himself.
He climbed up to the top of Spider Rock.

The young man took a rest in that beautiful place.
When he looked down, his enemy was gone.

The young man turned around and saw Spider Woman.
Her thread had saved him. She had tied one end to a rock.
Then she dropped the other end to the ground.

The peaceful young man said thank you.
Then he climbed down the thread and ran home.
He told his family how Spider Woman had saved him.

I Read Closely

Read. Mark the sentence that goes with the picture.

○ The young man took a rest in that beautiful place.

○ He wanted to climb the tall rock.

○ Then she made her home at the top of Spider Rock.

○ He climbed up to the top of Spider Rock.

○ He was being chased by an enemy.

○ Spider Rock is a tall, tall rock in a canyon.

○ He told his family how Spider Woman had saved him.

○ She had tied one end to a rock.

Name: _____

I Read and Understand

....

Read and answer.

1. Spider Rock is ____.
   ○ magic
   ○ tall

2. The young man was ____.
   ○ peaceful
   ○ an enemy

3. Spider Woman dropped a ____ thread.
   ○ young
   ○ magic

4. The young man ____ up Spider Rock.
   ○ climbed
   ○ tied

5. The thread saved the young man from his ____.
   ○ enemy
   ○ canyon

Name: _____

I Tell the Story

Finish the pictures. Tell someone the story.

1 Draw the rock.

2 Draw the thread.

3 Draw the spider.

4 Draw the fire.

I told the story to _____.

Reading Literary Text • EMC 3211 • © Evan-Moor Corp.

Name: _____

I Read a Folk Tale

A folk tale is a made-up story.
Sometimes the characters are animals.
The story may be about a real place or thing.
It may have magic in it, too.

Setting

1. Where does the story take place?

_____

Magic

2. Which thing was magic?

_____

Problem

3. What problem did the young man have?

   ○ He needed to make beautiful cloth.

   ○ An enemy was chasing him.

4. How was the young man saved?

   ○ He ran home.

   ○ He climbed up Spider Rock.

Name: _____

I Can Write

Write the words to finish each sentence.

Word Box

said thank you	the tall rock
by an enemy	saw Spider Woman

1. A young man was chased _____.

2. He wanted to climb _____.

3. He turned around and _____.

4. The peaceful young man _____.

Write your own sentence. Tell where the story takes place.

5. _____

_____

_____

_____

Answer Key

TE = Teacher's Edition
SB = Student Book

Unit 1

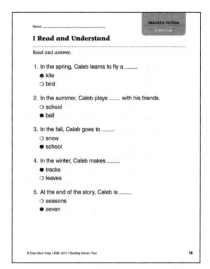

I Read Closely

Read. Mark the sentence that goes with the picture.

- ○ Squirrels are at work.
- ● Baby birds learn to fly.

- ○ The seasons come and go.
- ● Caleb makes tracks, too.

- ● Caleb does his work in school.
- ○ Animals make tracks in the snow.

- ● And now, Caleb is seven.
- ○ Summer days are long.

TE Page 18 / SB Page 12

I Read and Understand

Read and answer.

1. In the spring, Caleb learns to fly a ____.
   - ● kite
   - ○ bird

2. In the summer, Caleb plays ____ with his friends.
   - ○ school
   - ● ball

3. In the fall, Caleb goes to ____.
   - ○ snow
   - ● school

4. In the winter, Caleb makes ____.
   - ● tracks
   - ○ leaves

5. At the end of the story, Caleb is ____.
   - ○ seasons
   - ● seven

TE Page 19 / SB Page 13

I Tell the Story

Finish the pictures. Tell someone the story.

1 Draw the kite. 2 Draw the ball.
3 Draw Caleb. 4 Draw the tracks.

I told the story to ___ Answers will vary.

TE Page 20 / SB Page 14

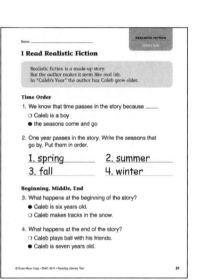

I Read Realistic Fiction

Realistic fiction is a made-up story.
But the author makes it seem like real life.
In "Caleb's Year" the author has Caleb grow older.

Time Order

1. We know that time passes in the story because ____
   - ○ Caleb is a boy
   - ● the seasons come and go

2. One year passes in the story. Write the seasons that go by. Put them in order.
   1. spring   2. summer
   3. fall   4. winter

Beginning, Middle, End

3. What happens at the beginning of the story?
   - ● Caleb is six years old.
   - ○ Caleb makes tracks in the snow.

4. What happens at the end of the story?
   - ○ Caleb plays ball with his friends.
   - ● Caleb is seven years old.

TE Page 21 / SB Page 15

I Can Write

Write the words to finish each sentence.

Word Box
are long   fall, and winter
come and go   cold

1. The seasons come and go
2. Summer days are long
3. Winter is cold
4. First comes spring, then summer, fall, and winter

Write your own sentence. Tell about one of the seasons.

5. Sample answer: Caleb plays ball in summer.

TE Page 22 / SB Page 16

Unit 2

I Read Closely

Read. Mark the sentence that goes with the picture. Then color.

- ● What is yellow?
- ○ What is orange?

- ● What is pink?
- ○ What is red?

- ○ What is violet?
- ● What is white?

- ○ What is blue?
- ● What is orange?

TE Page 32 / SB Page 28

I Read and Understand

Read and answer.

1. The name of the poem is ____.
   - ○ Pink
   - ● Color

2. A rose is pink by a fountain's ____.
   - ● brink
   - ○ cloud

3. The ____ is blue where the clouds float through.
   - ○ swan
   - ● sky

4. Clouds are violet in the summer ____.
   - ○ barley
   - ● twilight

5. What is orange? Just an ____!
   - ● orange
   - ○ pears

TE Page 33 / SB Page 29

I Remember the Poem

Finish the sentences. Tell someone the poem.

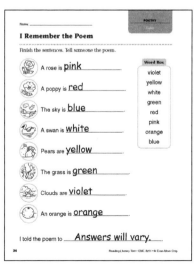

A rose is **pink**
A poppy is **red**
The sky is **blue**
A swan is **white**
Pears are **yellow**
The grass is **green**
Clouds are **violet**
An orange is **orange**

Word Box
violet
yellow
white
green
red
pink
orange
blue

I told the poem to ___ Answers will vary.

TE Page 34 / SB Page 30

I Read a Poem

A poem is a group of words that tell about an idea or a feeling.
Poems may have a pattern.
Poems may have rhyme.

Idea

1. The poem tells about ____.
   - ● many colors
   - ○ one color

Words That Rhyme

2. Read the sentence. Circle two words that rhyme.
   A swan is (white) sailing in the (light).

Words, Words, Words

3. Write the missing words in the pattern.
   What is green? The **grass** is green.
   What is white? A **swan** is white.
   What is yellow? **Pears** are yellow.

TE Page 35 / SB Page 31

Evan-Moor Corp. • EMC 3211 • Reading Literary Text   **121**

Unit 2 continued

TE Page 36 / SB Page 32

TE Page 46 / SB Page 44

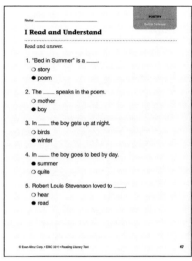

TE Page 47 / SB Page 45

TE Page 48 / SB Page 46

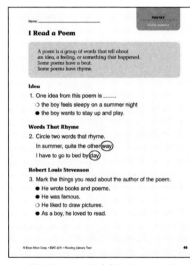

TE Page 49 / SB Page 47

TE Page 50 / SB Page 48

Unit 4

TE Page 60 / SB Page 60

TE Page 61 / SB Page 61

TE Page 62 / SB Page 62

Unit 4 continued

TE Page 63 / SB Page 63

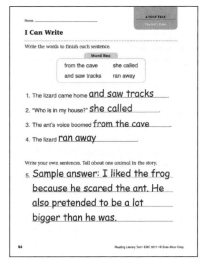

TE Page 64 / SB Page 64

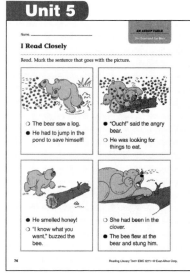

TE Page 74 / SB Page 76

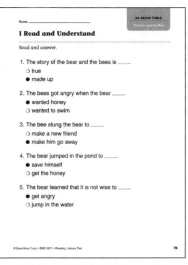

TE Page 75 / SB Page 77

TE Page 76 / SB Page 78

TE Page 77 / SB Page 79

TE Page 78 / SB Page 80

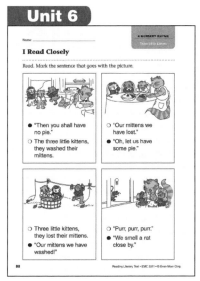

TE Page 88 / SB Page 92

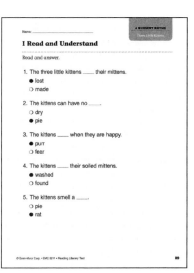

TE Page 89 / SB Page 93

TE Page 90 / SB Page 94

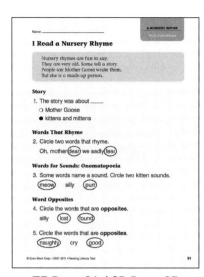

TE Page 91 / SB Page 95

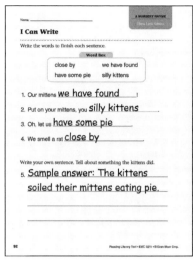

TE Page 92 / SB Page 96

Unit 7

TE Page 102 / SB Page 108

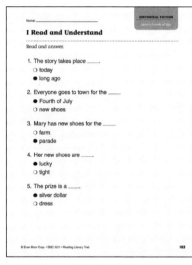

TE Page 103 / SB Page 109

TE Page 104 / SB Page 110

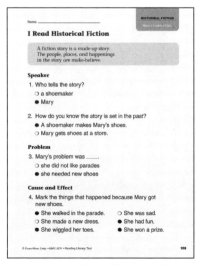

TE Page 105 / SB Page 111

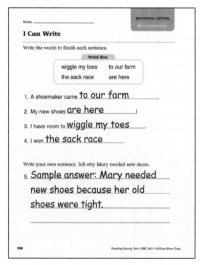

TE Page 106 / SB Page 112

Unit 8

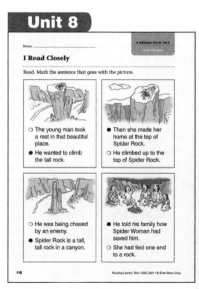

TE Page 116 / SB Page 124

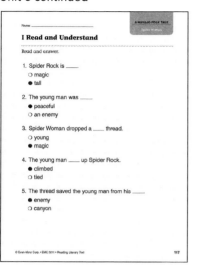

TE Page 117 / SB Page 125

TE Page 118 / SB Page 126

TE Page 119 / SB Page 127

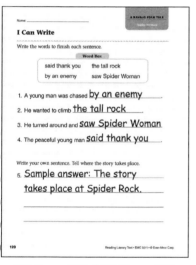

TE Page 120 / SB Page 128

Common Core Lessons

Reading Informational Text

Grade **1**

SAMPLER

Science
We Need the Sun

Lesson Objective Students will understand that living things need the sun's light and heat.

Content Knowledge The sun is an energy source for living things.

Lesson Preparation

Reproduce and distribute to each student one copy of the dictionary page (p. 11), the minibook pages (pp. 12–15), and the activity pages (pp. 16–19).

Student Minibook: Reproduce the minibook pages. Cut them in half and staple them together in numerical order to make an 8-page booklet.

Learn

1 Build Background

2 Introduce the Vocabulary
Dictionary

3 Read the Texts
We Need the Sun Minibook
Teacher's Complex Text

Analyze

4 Reading Comprehension Activities
I Read and Understand
I Read Closely

5 Close Reading Activity
Oral Discussion Questions

6 Vocabulary Activity
Words I Know

Write

7 Writing Activity
I Can Write

1 Build Background

Explain to students that Earth is a planet. It takes Earth 365 days to travel around the sun; that is one year. The sun is an ordinary star, but to us it looks bigger and brighter than all the billions of other stars in space. That is because it is much closer to Earth. An object that is closer looks bigger.

2 Introduce the Vocabulary

Content Vocabulary Point to each pictured word. Read the word aloud and have students echo you. Then have them write the word on the line. Explain any phonetic structures that are unfamiliar to your students. Discuss word meanings as needed.

Words to Know Point to each word and read it aloud. Have students echo you. Point out that the word *live* can mean "to stay alive" or "to make a home in a place."

CCSS: **RIT** 1.1, 1.2, 1.3, 1.4, 1.6, 1.7   **W** 1.2, 1.8   **SL** 1.1, 1.1c

3 Read the Texts

Minibook Guide students in reading the minibook together aloud.

Teacher's Complex Text Have students look at the pictures in their minibooks as you read aloud the corresponding Teacher's Complex Text on page 10. Say: *Look at the pictures in your book as I read you more information about why we need the sun. Look at the picture on page 1. Listen as I read.*

4 Reading Comprehension Activities

Guide students through completing the activities on pages 16 and 17. Encourage them to look in their minibooks to find information.

5 Close Reading Activity

Oral Discussion Use the Oral Discussion Questions on the right to guide students in a discussion about what they have read and heard. Before you begin, make sure each student has colored pencils and his or her minibook.

Begin by reading aloud a question and having students answer the question and mark the answer in their minibooks.

6 Vocabulary Activity

Guide students through the vocabulary activity on page 18. After they finish, have them draw and color a sun and write the word *sun* below it.

7 Writing Activity

Guide students through the writing activity on page 19. Have them use information from their minibook and the Teacher's Complex Text. Their sentences should relate to the story. Then have volunteers read aloud their sentences.

Oral Discussion Questions

1. **What is the title of the book?** (*We Need the Sun*) **Draw an orange box around it.** (title page)

2. **The sun is important to people on Earth. What two things does the sun give us?** (*light, heat*) **Circle the words with red.** (page 2)

3. **Why is light important to us?** (*The light of the sun helps us see.*) **Draw a green line under the word that tells what the sun helps us do.** (*see*) (page 3)

4. **Why is heat important to us?** (*The heat of the sun keeps us warm.*) **Draw a blue line under the word that tells how the sun makes us feel.** (*warm*) (page 4)

5. **How does the light of the sun help plants?** (*It helps them grow.*) **Color the sun on this page yellow.** (page 5)

6. **How do plants help animals?** (*They are food for animals.*) **Read aloud the sentence that tells you this.** (*Animals eat plants for food.*) **Draw a green line under the sentence.** (page 6)

7. **In order to have food, people need the sun. Why?** (*The sun helps plants grow. Animals eat the plants. People eat food from the plants and animals.*) **Color the people and the sun on page 7.**

We Need the Sun

The sun is a star. We think of stars twinkling at night in the dark sky. Those stars are very far away from Earth. The sun is a star, too, but it is much closer to Earth. When we see the sun shining during the day, it is so bright that we cannot see the other stars. The sun is our day star. It is a very important star to Earth.

Minibook, page 1

The sun gives us light and heat. The sun is a ball of hot gases. It makes energy inside, at its center. The energy moves out into space. We see the sun's energy as light. We feel the sun's energy as heat. On hot days, we protect our bodies from the sun's energy. We cover up with clothes or sunscreen. We wear sun hats.

Minibook, page 2

The light of the sun helps us see. Our eyes see best in the light. The sun is always shining, but at night we do not see its light. Because Earth turns, at night we are turned away from the sun. If the sun did not shine, the whole earth would be dark. There would be no day.

Minibook, page 3

The heat of the sun keeps us warm. We can feel the heat of the sun when we are outdoors. We can feel the heat of the sun when we are inside a car. If the sun did not shine, the whole earth would always be cold.

Minibook, page 4

The light of the sun helps plants grow. The sun is important to green plants. Plants use the sun's energy. They use air, water, and sunlight to make their own food. Plants cannot live without the sun.

Minibook, page 5

Animals eat plants for food. Cows eat grass, which is a plant. Monkeys eat the fruit of plants. Birds eat the seeds of plants. People eat grains, fruits, vegetables, nuts, and seeds, too. Living things need plants for their food.

Minibook, page 6

People eat plants for food. People eat meat, eggs, and milk that come from animals, too. Without plants and animals, people would not have food. Living things on Earth need the sun in order to live.

Minibook, page 7

Name: _____

Dictionary

Look at the picture. Read the word.
Write the word on the line.

Content Vocabulary

animals

_____

food

_____

grow

_____

light

_____

people

_____

plants

_____

star

_____

sun

_____

Words to Know

heat	keeps	live
need	night	warm

We Need the Sun

Name: _____

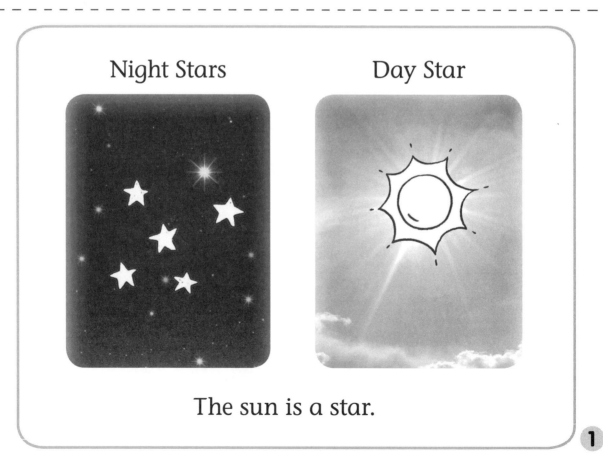

Night Stars

Day Star

The sun is a star.

1

The sun gives us light and heat.

2

The light of the sun helps us see.

3

The heat of the sun keeps us warm.

4

The light of the sun helps plants grow.

5

Animals eat plants for food.

6

People eat plants. People eat food from animals. We need the sun to live.

7

Reading Informational Text • EMC 3201 • © Evan-Moor Corp.

I Read and Understand

Read and answer.

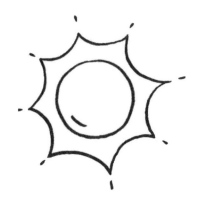

1. The sun is a ____.
   - ○ moon
   - ○ star

2. The sun gives us light and ____.
   - ○ heat
   - ○ earth

3. The sun helps plants ____.
   - ○ give
   - ○ grow

4. Plants are ____ for animals.
   - ○ food
   - ○ light

5. We need the ____ to live.
   - ○ people
   - ○ sun

Name: _____

SCIENCE

We Need the Sun

I Read Closely

Read. Mark the sentence that goes with the picture.

○ The sun is a night star.

○ The light of the sun helps us see.

○ Animals eat plants for food.

○ The heat of the sun keeps us warm.

○ Plants and animals need food.

○ The sun gives us light and heat.

○ We need the sun to live.

○ The sun helps plants grow.

Words I Know

Read and answer.

1. Our sun is a ____.
   - ○ food
   - ○ people
   - ○ star

2. ____ are food.
   - ○ Star
   - ○ Plants
   - ○ Keeps

3. We ____ on Earth.
   - ○ warm
   - ○ night
   - ○ live

4. ____ eat plants.
   - ○ Plants
   - ○ Animals
   - ○ Need

5. Heat keeps us ____.
   - ○ warm
   - ○ light
   - ○ people

I Can Write

Write the words to finish the sentence.

Word Box

need the sun	a day star
and heat	plants grow

1. The sun is _____.

2. The sun gives us light _____.

3. The sun helps _____.

4. People _____.

Write a sentence. Tell one thing the sun gives us.

_____

_____

Sampler Answer Key

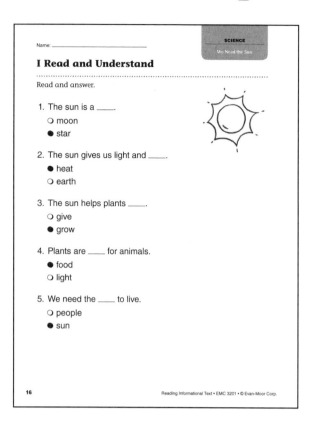

Page 16

Page 17

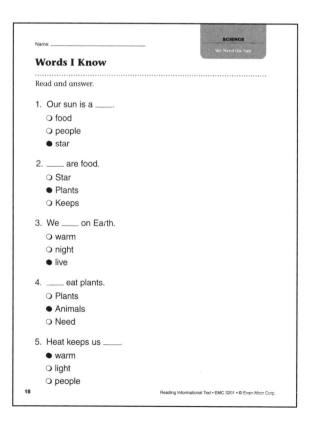

Page 18

Page 19

Stories to Read Words to Know

Student Book

Teacher's Guide

Audio CD

Foster a love of reading for English Language Learners in your classroom.

Stories to Read—Words to Know
Support ELLs in the mainstream classroom.

Rich with colorful illustrations and creative content, this series will help ELL students develop language skills through reading. Provide students with meaningful opportunities to read, and encourage reluctant readers with an audio of the story so they can follow along.

Federal funding sources: I, III   **evan-moor.com/storiestoread**

Each *Stories to Read—Words to Know* Starter Kit contains:

Student Book	Full-color storybook provides students with the motivation and practice they need to master language skills. 96 pages. • 12 full-color stories • Picture dictionaries • Activity pages that target important skills
Teacher's Guide	Step-by-step lesson plans and additional teaching resources make it easy to guide students through each lesson. 64 pages. • Reading strategies • Guided instruction • Oral language practice • Vocabulary practice strips • Assessment tests
Audio CD	Engaging audio readings support struggling or reluctant readers as they follow along with the story. Audio selections are also available in downloadable podcasts on iTunes.

Book	Reading Grade Level
A	K
B	K
C	K–1
D	1
E	1
F	1–2
G	2
H	2–3
I	3
J	3

Complete Set
Includes all 10 Starter Kits.

Complete Set   EMC 3340

Starter Kit

Book A	EMC 3666	Book F	EMC 3671
Book B	EMC 3667	Book G	EMC 3672
Book C	EMC 3668	Book H	EMC 3673
Book D	EMC 3669	Book I	EMC 3674
Book E	EMC 3670	Book J	EMC 3675

Student Book 5-Pack

Book A	EMC 3681	Book F	EMC 3686
Book B	EMC 3682	Book G	EMC 3687
Book C	EMC 3683	Book H	EMC 3688
Book D	EMC 3684	Book I	EMC 3689
Book E	EMC 3685	Book J	EMC 3690

Individual Student Book

Book A	EMC 3466	Book F	EMC 3471
Book B	EMC 3467	Book G	EMC 3472
Book C	EMC 3468	Book H	EMC 3473
Book D	EMC 3469	Book I	EMC 3474
Book E	EMC 3470	Book J	EMC 3475

Get daily reading comprehension practice into your curriculum!

Daily Reading Comprehension

Supplement your reading instruction and prepare students for state testing with 150 daily lessons. In just 10 to 15 minutes a day, *Daily Reading Comprehension* presents students with the reading strategies and skills they need to become successful lifetime readers! 192 pages. ***Correlated to state and Common Core State Standards.***

You'll love *Daily Reading Comprehension* because it…

- includes 150 original fiction and nonfiction passages accompanied by follow-up comprehension activities

- includes teacher pages with suggestions and ideas for guiding students through each passage

- provides instruction and practice on six reading strategies, such as asking questions and determining importance, and 12 important skills, such as cause and effect and nonfiction text features.

DAILY READING COMPREHENSION

Grade Level	Teacher's Reproducible Edition	Student Pack (5 Student Books)	Class Pack (20 Student Books + Teacher's Edition)
1	EMC 3451	EMC 6631	EMC 9691
2	EMC 3452	EMC 6632	EMC 9692
3	EMC 3453	EMC 6633	EMC 9693
4	EMC 3454	EMC 6634	EMC 9694
5	EMC 3455	EMC 6635	EMC 9695
6	EMC 3456	EMC 6636	EMC 9696
7	EMC 3457	EMC 6637	EMC 9697
8	EMC 3458	EMC 6638	EMC 9698

Perfect Supplements to Your Core Curriculum!

Research Based

Daily Language Review, Common Core Edition

Each book provides four or five items for every day of a 36-week school year. Skill areas include grammar, punctuation, mechanics, usage, and sentence editing. There are also scope and sequence charts, suggestions for use, and answer keys for the teacher. 136 pages.

Correlated to state and Common Core State Standards.

Teacher's Edition		Student Pack (5 Student Books)		Class Pack (20 Student Books + Teacher's Edition)	
Grade 1	EMC 579	Grade 1	EMC 6515	Grade 1	EMC 6521
Grade 2	EMC 580	Grade 2	EMC 6516	Grade 2	EMC 6522
Grade 3	EMC 581	Grade 3	EMC 6517	Grade 3	EMC 6523
Grade 4	EMC 582	Grade 4	EMC 6518	Grade 4	EMC 6524
Grade 5	EMC 583	Grade 5	EMC 6519	Grade 5	EMC 6525
Grade 6	EMC 576	Grade 6	EMC 6520	Grade 6	EMC 6526
Grade 7	EMC 2797	Grade 7	EMC 6597	Grade 7	EMC 9677
Grade 8	EMC 2798	Grade 8	EMC 6598	Grade 8	EMC 9678

Research Based

Daily Math Practice, Common Core Edition

Grade appropriate, educationally sound, and designed to support your math curriculum. Based on NCTM standards, *Daily Math Practice, Common Core Edition* addresses key learning objectives including computation, problem solving, reasoning, geometry, measurement, and much more. Answer key and scope and sequence chart included. 128 pages.

Correlated to state and Common Core State Standards.

Teacher's Edition		Student Pack (5 Student Books)		Class Pack (20 Student Books + Teacher's Edition)	
Grade 1	EMC 750	Grade 1	EMC 6527	Grade 1	EMC 6533
Grade 2	EMC 751	Grade 2	EMC 6528	Grade 2	EMC 6534
Grade 3	EMC 752	Grade 3	EMC 6529	Grade 3	EMC 6535
Grade 4	EMC 753	Grade 4	EMC 6530	Grade 4	EMC 6536
Grade 5	EMC 754	Grade 5	EMC 6531	Grade 5	EMC 6537
Grade 6	EMC 755	Grade 6	EMC 6532	Grade 6	EMC 6538

Successful Students Practice at Home!

AWARD-WINNING*

SKILL SHARPENERS

PreK–6

Connecting School & Home

Skill Sharpeners provides at-home practice that helps students master and retain skills. Each book in this dynamic series is the ideal resource for programs such as summer school, after school, remediation, school book fairs, and fundraising. 144 full-color pages.

- **activities aligned with national and state standards**
- **assessment pages in standardized-test format**
- **full-color, charmingly illustrated, and kid-friendly**

Spell & Write

PreK	EMC 4535	3	EMC 4539
K	EMC 4536	4	EMC 4540
1	EMC 4537	5	EMC 4541
2	EMC 4538	6	EMC 4542

Reading

PreK	EMC 4527	3	EMC 4531
K	EMC 4528	4	EMC 4532
1	EMC 4529	5	EMC 4533
2	EMC 4530	6	EMC 4534

Math

PreK	EMC 4543	3	EMC 4547
K	EMC 4544	4	EMC 4548
1	EMC 4545	5	EMC 4549
2	EMC 4546	6	EMC 4550

Science

PreK	EMC 5319	3	EMC 5323
K	EMC 5320	4	EMC 5324
1	EMC 5321	5	EMC 5325
2	EMC 5322	6	EMC 5326

"Colorful and fun! **Skill Sharpeners** *has successfully engaged my very easily distracted son. I highly recommend it."*

—Parent, Cambridge, Idaho

The National Parenting Center, Seal of Approval Winner

iParenting Media Awards Outstanding Product